What's a Kid Like Me Doing in a Family Like This?

K A R E N ▼ D O C K R E Y

> Student books
> are available for use
> in group study.

VICTOR BOOKS®
A DIVISION OF SCRIPTURE PRESS PUBLICATIONS INC.
USA CANADA ENGLAND

Other SonPower Small Group Studies
Can We Talk, God? (devotional life)
Can't Fight the Feelings (emotions)
Why Not Love All of Me? (whole-person relationships)
Where Do You Think Sex Came From? (sexuality)

Scripture quotations, unless otherwise indicated, are from the *Holy Bible, New International Version,* © 1973, 1978, 1984, International Bible Society. Used by permission of Zondervan Bible Publishers. Verses marked NASB are from the *New American Standard Bible,* © the Lockman Foundation 1960, 1962, 1963, 1968, 1971, 1972, 1973, 1975, 1977. Verses marked TLB are taken from *The Living Bible,* © 1971, Tyndale House Publishers, Wheaton, IL 60189. Verses marked ICV are quoted from the *International Children's Bible, New Century Version,* © 1986, 1988 by Word Publishing, Dallas, Texas 75039. Used by permission. Verses marked KJV are quoted from the *Authorized (King James) Version.*

Copyediting: Lin Johnson
Cover Design: Mardelle Ayres
Cover Photos: Jonathan Meyers, Jim Whitmer
Interior Illustrations: Marilee Harrold Pilz

ISBN: 0-89693-113-7

1 2 3 4 5 6 7 8 9 10   Printing/Year 96 95 94 93 92

© 1992, SP Publications, Inc. All rights reserved.
Printed in the United States of America.

No part of this book may be reproduced without written permission, except for brief quotations in books and critical reviews. For information write Victor Books, 1825 College Avenue, Wheaton, Illinois 60187.

CONTENTS

Introduction   5

1 It's the Little Things That Get You   9
Caring choices at home can make families happier

2 They're Always on My Back   21
Working with parents on goals can turn destructive pressure into creative pressure

3 Why Can't My Parents Understand?   36
Developing understanding skills can grow closeness with parents

4 Give Me Roots So I Can Fly   48
Asking parents for what we need and thanking them for what they have given us promotes greater security

5 They Love Her More Than Me   60
Asking family members to accept us as we are and treating them likewise promotes family unity

6 I'll Tell You What My Parents Think about God   73
We can grow spiritually no matter what our parents' relationship with God is like

ABOUT THE AUTHOR

KAREN DOCKREY has worked with teens and their leaders for over 17 years. She served two churches as minister of youth and currently spends her professional time writing for teens and their leaders. Her 14 books include *Family Survival Guide* and *The Youth Worker's Guide to Creative Bible Study* (both Victor Books). She earned a Master of Divinity degree from Southern Baptist Theological Seminary and presently works with youth at Bluegrass Baptist Church in Hendersonville, Tennessee.

INTRODUCTION

Small Group Studies

This small group study is designed to guide group members to grow in their personal relationships with Christ as expressed in their families. A small group format provides unique opportunities to do so. A small group is a group of 4–12 people who meet together regularly for the shared purpose of pursuing and living biblical truth. They seek to mature in Christ and become equipped to serve as His ministers in the world. As group members commit to six weeks of study, this book will guide them to discover and live God's truth through:

>Bible searching,
>>honest sharing,
>>>receptive listening,
>>>>supportive caring.

As is true for all the Small Group studies, the small group setting and the format of this book make it possible for group members to (1) provide Jesus-based acceptance for each other; (2) challenge each other with God's truth;

(3) offer supportive community to strengthen personal and spiritual growth and to encourage each other to be all God has called them to be.

Guide your group members to agree on and commit to these purposes. Just as the Christian community grew, served one another, and served the larger community as equipped by God (Acts 2; 1 Corinthians 12; Ephesians 4), so your small group can experience the reality of the body of Christ.

Contemporary adolescent culture offers little opportunity for interpersonal intimacy, honesty, safety, healing, or growth. In a Christian small group, teens can take off their masks, find acceptance, receive encouragement to grow, and discover ways to serve. In turn, they can give these gifts to other group members. Also, in small groups, adolescents can search together for meaningful answers to their questions.

The only prerequisite for joining a small group is a heart willing to develop relationships with friends and with Jesus Christ. Many groups find it helpful to write and sign covenants that promise confidentiality, attendance unless providentially hindered, and steady love.

In each session you'll find these features:

SESSION OVERVIEW

The elements in this section provide a summary of the small group focus for the session. At quick glance you can discover the purpose, needs, goals, and desired results of the session.

Purpose states the intent of the session, defining the central reason for this small group experience.

Needs examines adolescents themselves and why they need this small group experience.

Goals lists objectives for both the leader and group mem-

INTRODUCTION

bers. These goals provide an opportunity to focus the session, adapt it, and evaluate its effectiveness. If you aim at nothing, you'll hit it. This section helps you hit your target.

Life Response suggests a specific commitment each group member can make to live out God's truth during the week. Additional suggestions for groups with higher commitment levels follow each session.

Resource Materials lists what you need for the session.

Pacing suggests how much time to spend on each section.

 HEARTBEAT

These opening experiences take a pulse and get to the heart of who and where students are. This section is experiential, not something you tell or teach. Honest sharing, active listening, and accurate affirmation are key to this first step toward community building. This section focuses group members on the question, **"Who am I?"**

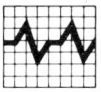 **LIFELINE**

The main part of the small group experience is studying God's Word. During this section, students move from where they are to where God wants them to be. During this time, guide group members to discover God's truth for themselves as they ask, **"Who am I called to be?"**

 BODYLIFE

To close the session, group members experience the reality of Christ as they commit themselves individually and corporately to be all God calls them to be. This section focuses group members on the question, **"What action will I take in the light of God's Word?"**

7

HINTS & HELPS

☞ **HELPS** provide insights and resources to address student concerns and questions. They provide Bible insight, sample answers, and other information.

☞ **HINTS** provide small group leadership skills. These points of advice help you lead specific exercises or encourage closeness and support in the group.

GROUP MEMBER AND LEADER MATERIALS

Group members' workbooks include the main content of the HEARTBEAT, LIFELINE, and BODYLIFE sections of each session. This same content is reproduced in your leader's edition with additional exercises and activities printed in **boldface.**

PREPARATION

Read each session through and become familiar with the purposes, needs, and goals. Then adapt the content to meet the specific needs of your group.

Some groups may need added emphasis on the HEARTBEART, LIFELINE, or BODYLIFE sections. These needs may change from session to session. The sessions are written to accommodate the greater closeness and comfort that develop. Let prayer guide your preparation, your session leading, and your follow-through.

Group members are not required to prepare ahead of time. But as the LIFELINE and BODYLIFE sections impact lives, they will want to share their discoveries and obedience. Doing so provides opportunity for accountability and support.

ONE

It's the Little Things That Get You

SESSION OVERVIEW

Purpose:
The purpose of this six-week study is to guide group members to grow in their personal relationships with Christ as expressed in their families. This session focuses on the choices family members make to care or curse in little ways.

Needs:
Closeness between teenagers and their parents is created or destroyed by daily actions. It doesn't just happen. Too often, family members curse instead of care. They don't mean to hurt anyone; they just don't think ahead. Or they think their actions don't matter. When even one family member recognizes the impact of little actions, he or she can create a more caring family.

Just as family *closeness* can come through one member's actions, so can family *carelessness*. Adolescents as well as adults are guilty of dividing families. Some stay too busy to listen, launch into lecture mode instead of listening, hog or interrupt phone conversations. This session encourages adolescents to improve their actions in this area.

WHAT'S A KID LIKE ME DOING IN A FAMILY LIKE THIS?

Goals:
The goals for the *leader* include
(1) creating an atmosphere of cooperation and belonging;
(2) guiding members to voice family gripes and goods;
(3) challenging group members to notice how the Bible's advice can solve problems and increase closeness;
(4) motivating group members to commit to caring choices in their families.

The goals for the *group members* are that they will
(1) empathize with one another's family situations;
(2) air gripes and discover good in the midst of them;
(3) discover biblical ways to solve gripes;
(4) commit to six weeks of study and to each other.

Life Response:
Group members will encourage one another to be positive forces in their families. Each group member will choose one thing he can do to make his family a happier unit.

Resource Materials:
___ Bibles
___ one copy of *What's a Kid Like Me Doing in a Family Like This?* (student book) for each group member
___ paper and pens or pencils
___ poster with sentence starters

Pacing:
Spend about 20 minutes each with HEARTBEAT, LIFELINE, and BODYLIFE. During later sessions you'll spend the most time on LIFELINE, but this first session requires extra time for group building and covenanting. If group members get to talking, all the activities may take longer than an hour. So pick three on which to focus and use the others to supplement as you have time.

IT'S THE LITTLE THINGS THAT GET YOU

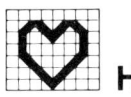 **HEARTBEAT**

Build the Group
Welcome each group member warmly as he or she enters. Display these four sentence starters.
- My favorite thing about school is. . . .
- In my free time I like to. . . .
- My favorite TV show is. . . .
- In five years I want to be. . . .

Invite each member to complete three accurately and one inaccurately. Let the group guess which sentence is wrong. Be certain to participate yourself.

Picture the Truth
Give everyone a piece of clay to shape to show an ideal family. Explain that the sculpture can be a symbol, characteristic, person, or something else. Encourage and affirm ideas as they emerge. Assure group members that there is no one correct answer.

☞ [HINT: Though they may balk initially, young adults enjoy shaping clay. It enables them to express complex truths in visual form. Clay has added advantages for the first session because group members feel less anxious as they squeeze the clay. If group members wonder why they are shaping clay, explain these reasons.]

Call for group members to tell about their sculptures, beginning with volunteers. Name a valuable insight in each. Write descriptive words or phrases on a chalkboard or paper so all group members can read them. (Examples include: A family understands; helps me feel at home; does things together; trusts; is always there; believes in each other; belongs.)

Agree that no family is this perfect, but these ideals can be goals to strive for. Point out that during this

11

session and this series, we'll discover ways to bring our present and future families closer to this ideal.

☞ [HINT: Allow group members to keep the clay during the session on these conditions: They may not throw or pass it, and it must stay in one piece. As they squeeze and mold it, they focus on discussion.]

Guide group members to open their books to "My Calling in My Family" on page 7 and read the introductory paragraph. Ask everyone to share a favorite phrase from it.

Direct them to write or draw their first reactions to the three questions. Because the clay sculpting explored question 1, suggest they recall and jot down their favorite insights from the sculpting experience. As members finish, guide them to underline three phrases in the introduction on pages 5 and 6 that apply most closely to them. Then share responses, encouraging active listening and allowing no put-downs.

My Calling in My Family

Relationships count. Good relationships give the security, belonging, experiences, and ideas you need to be happy and whole. This is precisely why family is so important. As you and God explore the strengths and weaknesses in your family, you'll discover how to grow a closer family. As you and other group members show understanding and encouragement for one another, you'll find power to live out the actions and attitudes you discover. As a bonus, you'll learn to create closeness outside your family.

What does the ideal family look like? Sound like? Feel like? Smell like? Taste like?

How does your family compare to this ideal? Name one way your family meets the ideal and one way it falls short.

IT'S THE LITTLE THINGS THAT GET YOU

God cares about your family and what happens in it. What do you think is God's calling for you in your family? (A calling is what God wants you to accomplish, learn, or do.)

As an emerging adult, your family needs are changing. During this study, we'll explore the new ways you need your family, the new ways your family needs you, and how to ask for and grow these kinds of closeness. During it all, listen for God's will for you in your family.

☞ **[HINT: The purpose of HEARTBEAT is to build community and identify the members' needs. Rather than try to answer all the needs and questions right now, focus on understanding. Jot group members' needs down, explaining that you will use them to custom design the study. Highlight places in the six sessions where their needs are addressed.]**

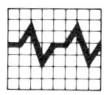 **LIFELINE**
Little Things Make a Big Difference
The needs you identified in the previous section won't be granted with the wave of a wand. They take consistent little actions in big areas—areas like expressed concern, genuine interest, caring communication, effective problem solving, and being considerate.

Write or draw four little things that make a big difference according to James 3:3-6. What does each control?

Little thing   *What it controls*

1.

2.

3.

4.

WHAT'S A KID LIKE ME DOING IN A FAMILY LIKE THIS?

☞ **[HELP: Rudders guide huge ships, bits control horses, sparks start fires, the tongue controls the whole person. Focus group members on the tongue.]**

What happens in your family when you (or another family member) don't control your tongue?

What happens if you control it too much (hold in anger, frustration, confusion, pain, and other feelings)?

What happens when you say what you feel, think, and want with kindness?

One little tongue controls communication (or lack of it), sharing experiences (or lack of it), and showing care (or neglecting to show it). These make (or break) your family. Read James 3:9-10. Caring for God means caring for people. Family closeness is important not just for its own sake but also because it shows care for God.

Circle the little tongue action that could make the biggest difference in your family and tell how.

Consider feelings.
  Listen instead of jump to conclusions.
    Show genuine interest.
      Say "I'm sorry."
        Take time to talk with each other.
          Accept each other as valuable and interesting individuals.
            Be kindly honest.
              Solve problems together.
                Other: _____

How I Respond to Little Things
You can't control the decisions of your parents or siblings. What you *can* control is the way you respond to others'

decisions. You also control the decisions you make.

Focus on reactions for a moment. What do these verses say about how your reactions affect the other person?

Proverbs 14:29 —

☞ [HELP: Ask: How does understanding impact the way you respond to uncaring actions? (Example: You understand that your mom yells because she's worried about your sick sister.) How does understanding impact the way you give attention? (Example: As you talk away, your dad understands you want to tell every detail. He listens rather than calls you a chatterbox.)]

☞ [HINT: If your group is larger than four, divide into cell groups of two or three for the other passages. This allows time for each person to share details.]

James 1:19 —

☞ [HELP: Invite members to notice how this Scripture works by asking: What happens when family members are quicker to speak than to listen? Quicker to become angry than to listen? Quicker to listen than to speak? Quicker to listen than to become angry?]

Proverbs 15:18 —

☞ [HELP: Draw out how this Scripture works by saying: Share a time you or a family member calmed a quarrel rather than stirred it up. How did it help? Tell about a time you or a family member made a quarrel worse. What words or actions would have worked better?]

Matthew 5:9 —

☞ **[HELP: Explain that peacemaking doesn't mean always backing off. It means doing whatever promotes closeness and understanding. Ask for actions and words that promote family peace. Encourage actions that promote true peace, not just absence of conflict.]**

The Little Things I Choose to Do
Recall two ways to create family closeness:
(1) Choose the way you respond to family members.
(2) Make your own wise action choices.

So far we've focused on responses. Now focus on choosing your own actions. Search Colossians 3:5-17, especially verses 8-10 and 12-15, for Paul's advice on living your faith with other people. Far from being idealistic advice for a perfectly cooperating family, Paul wrote this advice from prison to a church victimized by false teaching. How might personally practicing this advice bring your less-than-perfect family closer to God's ideal?

List the "rid yourself" actions from verses 5-9 on these discarded clothes. Write a way each would create family closeness if you removed it from your life.

IT'S THE LITTLE THINGS THAT GET YOU

Now list the "clothe yourself with" actions from verses 12-15 on these new clothes. Write a way each would add family closeness by adding it to your life.

Which "rid yourself" action can be replaced by which "clothe yourself" action? Many combinations are possible. Write at least three examples.
-
-
-
-

How might responding to a "rid yourself" action with a "clothe yourself" action work better than trying to retaliate? Give a specific example.

How might deliberately treating your family members with "clothe yourself" actions increase the happiness quotient in your home? Tell how you'll use a specific action.

☞ **[HELP: Point out that the Colossians had swallowed false teachings. Ask: What false teachings do our families face? (Example: If things get rough, they split.)**

What true teachings work better? (Example: Work things out, solve our problems.)]

 **BODYLIFE**

As you read through the "rid yourself" and "clothe yourself" actions, you likely thought of plenty that your parents could take off and put on. Rank your parents on the following continuum, using a D for your dad or stepdad and an M for your mom or stepmom. All but the first four items are specific examples from Colossians 3.

Rid yourself   *Clothe yourself*
Focus on my needs............Consider other's needs
Lecture..Listen
Demand..Give
Expect one to be like another......Accept each for self
Display anger and rage .... Display compassion
Show malice .... Show kindness
Slander...Love
Use filthy language .... Use kind words
Lie .... Be totally honest
Show pride .... Show humility
Be harsh .... Be gentle
Want change now .... Show patience
Complain .... Bear with one another
Hold grudges .... Forgive

If you were to give an award for the Best Dressed Family Member, using the "clothe yourself" characteristics as criteria, who would win in your family? Why?

☞   [HINT: Note the opportunity this gives to share about good in families and to specifically apply Scripture.]

Rank yourself with a Y on the above continuum. How similar are you and your parents? In what ways do you and

IT'S THE LITTLE THINGS THAT GET YOU

your parents already show care? Thank God for these. Where can you improve? How will you do so? How will doing the put-on actions help even if you are the only family member who does them?

☞ [HELP: Encourage group members to focus on *their* actions, since those are the only ones they can control.]

Life Response

Covenant with other group members to help each other be positive forces in your homes. Begin by committing to Christlikeness. Continue by obeying God in interaction with parents, siblings, and others. Use or adapt the following example. It spells LAFF (the result of family happiness).

☞ [HINT: Many groups like to compose their own covenants. Affirm that, because they are family in Christ, they can have many of the ideals of family: loyalty, standing up for each other, understanding, listening, and more. Include these in the covenant.]

Thank group members for commitment to God and to each other. Close by thanking God for a specific strength in each group member present.

☞ [HELP: Additional Life Responses to include if time allows or to suggest for follow-through at home:
1. Roleplay how actions in the continuum under BODYLIFE happen or could happen in your home. Begin with a negative, such as focusing on your needs. Then replay the same event, focusing on compassion rather than on your own needs. Use typical home conflicts like phone use or disagreements over curfew.
2. Journal how little actions led to the big problems in your home. Write about how little actions can solve those problems.]

> *Listen actively to understand and care.* Rather than press for my turn, I'll show interest in what you say and feel. Rather than assume my situation is like yours, I'll listen for details to help me understand.
>
> *Affirm sincerely.* I'll not only listen, but I'll accept and comment on what you say. I'll affirm (compliment) you when you do well in your family rather than cut you down when you blow it. I'll be sincere in my compliments so you can know I mean what I say.
>
> *Feel feelings.* I won't be afraid of my own or your family happiness, sadness, hope, and fear. As we feel one anothers' feelings and discover what those feelings mean, we enable each other to address life with godly action.
>
> *Faith response.* I'll make changes in my life based on God's Word. Obedience to God will determine how I act. I will encourage you to respond to God in family life. When I share ideas, I'll make them specific, biblical, and workable. Rather than general advice like "be Christlike," I'll offer specific words and actions Jesus might do.
>
> _____   _____
> (signature)   (date)

What's Next?

"They're Always on My Back"—What pressures do your parents put on you? When are these pressures helpful? When are they destructive?

TWO
▼

They're Always on My Back

SESSION OVERVIEW

Purpose:
This session explores the pressures parents place on adolescents. Some of these pressures are creative, such as encouragement to accomplish a goal. Others are destructive, such as expecting top standing in class or on a team. Group members will distinguish types of pressures, notice reasons parents do each, and discover ways to respond to both creative and destructive pressures with God's power.

Needs:
Some parents place extraordinary pressure on their adolescent children, expecting excellence in school, sports, and spirituality. Though most parents mean to encourage, this pressure often does the opposite; it makes adolescents feel powerless and worthless.

Some parents monitor the pressure they place on their adolescents, expecting the best and helping them achieve it. This becomes encouragement or guidance.

Learning to manage negative pressure and thrive under positive pressure is essential to emotional and spiritual survival. Dealing with pressure in families equips adolescents to manage the pressure of our high pressure age. God's power is the key to doing both.

Goals:
The goals for the *leader* include
(1) defining pressure as a potentially creative force that becomes dangerous when it is too great or too scant;
(2) guiding group members to turn to God for power to appreciate good pressure and cope with bad;
(3) guiding group members to cooperate with their parents to establish and work toward mutual goals.

The goals for the *group members* are that they will
(1) affirm some pressure as a creative force;
(2) access God's power for facing pressure;
(3) establish a pressure-response style that gives both stamina and rest;
(4) work with parents to choose and fulfill mutual goals.

Life Response:
Group members will identify ways to work with parents toward the same goals, making the most of creative pressure and changing destructive pressures.

Resource Materials:
___ Bibles
___ pens or pencils
___ one copy of *What's a Kid Like Me Doing in a Family Like This?* (student book) for each group member

Pacing:
For this and subsequent sessions, spend 10 minutes with HEARTBEAT, 20 with LIFELINE, and 10 with BODYLIFE. If group members show high interest in one or more sections, doing all the activities may take longer than an hour. Pick one from each section and use the others to supplement.

HEARTBEAT

Warm up the group by inviting them to give the weather report of their lives. Instruct them to include current conditions as well as a seven-day forecast. Suggest such details as temperature, skies, and travel conditions.

☞ [HINT: Encourage sensitive sharing by modeling it yourself. Allow no put-downs. Introduce any new members.]

Transition to the session by explaining that one indicator of coming weather is barometric pressure. Direct group members to open their books to notice how parental pressure can be like a pressure cooker and barometric pressure.

Creative or Destructive Pressure?
Parents can be the people who help us face the pressures in our lives, or they can be the main source of pressure. Before dismissing it as bad, notice that pressure from parents can be good, bad, or a combination of both. A pressure cooker and a barometer illustrate why.

Pressure Cooker
A pressure cooker needs just enough heat for just the right time to produce tender and tasty food. The heat produces the pressure that cooks the food—without the heat the food won't cook. But when the pressure gets too high, both the pressure cooker and the food inside explode.

Because a pressure cooker is sealed, no one can see the pressure or watch how well the food is cooking. Users must depend on a pressure indicator valve that tells them how much pressure is building and how fast.

WHAT'S A KID LIKE ME DOING IN A FAMILY LIKE THIS?

People are similar. No one can look at you and tell how much pressure you feel. But indicators like what you say and how you say it, fatigue, grouchiness, inability to concentrate, worry, anxiety, and anger show that too much pressure may be building. Indicators like joy, accomplishment, solved problems, and feelings of belonging show that you have just the right amount of pressure.

Compare yourself to a pressure cooker. Fill in the pressure cooker to the level that illustrates the amount of pressure you feel right now. Will it produce a healthier you or tend to destroy you? Why?

Pressure Cooker
Enough pressure to cook the food
to tasty perfection or enough to blow it up?

Barometer
A barometer measures changes in air pressure. When the air pressure changes, the weather changes along with it. Interestingly, low pressure indicates cloudy weather and high pressure indicates clear weather.

When might low pressure bring cloudiness to your life?

☞ **[HELP: Example: Parents who don't ask what's happening in your life or help you set limits can make you feel no one cares.]**

When might high pressure bring clear days?

☞ **[HELP: Example: A parent who encourages you to overcome your shyness by insisting that you speak to someone new every day gives you the pressure that brings friendship.]**

Circle the barometer below that most closely represents your life. Does the pressure from your family make your life cloudier or clearer? Why?

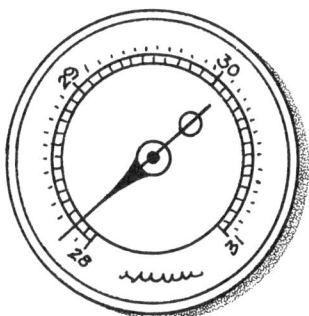

Barometer #1
Low pressure
indicating cloudy weather

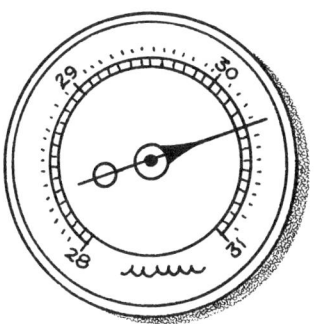

Barometer #2
High pressure
indicating clear weather

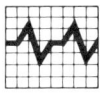 **LIFELINE**

When Pressure is Good

We need some pressure to motivate us to accomplish goals, to keep on with the good things in our lives, and to change our bad points. This good pressure is called encouragement. What does Hebrews 10:24-25 say about pressure?

List in the left column on the next page a pressure your parents place on you. In the right column, name a possible love or good deed your parents may be trying to encourage (Hebrews 10:24). A sample has been completed:

WHAT'S A KID LIKE ME DOING IN A FAMILY LIKE THIS?

Pressure	Love, good deed
Talk out problems rather than yell.	I keep friends & stay close to family members.

☞ [HINT: As group members complete this section, suggest they list all the pressures first and then move to the reasons. If they try to list a reason with every pressure, they may get bogged down and forget other pressures.]

When Pressure is Bad
Sometimes parents place pressures that cause more damage than harm. Because parents don't mean to cause harm, it may help to talk to them about how they affect you. Think about a painful pressure your parents place on you. What is the pressure, and what do you want to tell your parents about it?

☞ [HINT: As group members jot down their answers, write yours too. Your participation adds to the mutuality of the group.]

Give your parents the same understanding you want from them. What do you think makes your parent(s) pressure you? Check all reasons that apply.
- ☐ To look good so they can look good.
- ☐ To reach a dream they never reached.
- ☐ So you will be the best for your sake.
- ☐ They believe in your ability.
- ☐ They were pressured by a parent and know no other way.
- ☐ They want the best, smartest, and most capable kids.
- ☐ _____

Can you ask your parents why they pressure you? How does their motivation impact what you say to them about pressure?

In Any Pressure
As you and your parents work to understand each other, be assured that God always understands. Even better, He

has the power to help you through both fair and unfair pressures.

Read Isaiah 40:28-31. Complete these valuable truths:

- "Do you not know? Have you not heard? The Lord is _____."

☞ [HELP: *Answer:* "the everlasting God, the Creator of the ends of the earth." Focus on the fact that God is in touch with every element of every life and is intimately concerned with the details in group members' lives.]

- "He will not grow _____ or _____ and his _____ no one can fathom."

☞ [HELP: *Answer:* "tired, weary, understanding." Focus on the fact that God's energy, understanding, and power are limitless. When we're tired and feel we can't go on, He's not and He can.]

- "He gives _____."

☞ [HELP: *Answer:* "strength to the weary and increases the power of the weak." Assure group members that God not only has strength but gives it to us. He gives us all the power we need to face and triumph over our pressures. Whether our parents cooperate with God or not, God will help us triumph.]

- "Even youths grow _____."

☞ [HELP: *Answer:* "tired and weary." Emphasize that fatigue and feeling like you can't possibly get it all done are central problems with pressure. God understands this situation.]

Verses 28-30 stress that God's power is the solution to our tiredness, our pain, our weakness. Verse 31 explains what happens when we depend on His power:

- "Those who _____ in the Lord will renew their _____.
  They will _____.
  They will _____.
  They will _____."

Notice three results of depending on God: soaring, running, walking. None show any deeper faith than the others. All three express trust in God. All three give you strength and allow you to keep on going with joy.

☞ [HINT: If you have more than four members, divide into cell groups of two or three to share ideas on SOARing, RUNning, WALKing.]

SOAR—Some pressures are solved as easily as finishing that school project or talking with your parents. Name a pressure through which God has helped you or could help you to SOAR and how He did (or could) do it.

RUN—Some pressures are solved with steady, concentrated effort, like paying close attention during a tough class or continuing to work out expectations with your parents. Name a pressure through which God has helped you or could help you to RUN and how He did (or could) do it.

WALK—Some pressures go on and on, and we get through them step by step and with God's steady power. Examples include doing your homework regularly and reminding yourself that you are valuable even when your parents put you down daily. Name a pressure through which God has helped you or could help you to WALK and how He did (or could) do it.

☞ [HINT: Suggest chronic problems like a learning disability, a physical handicap, or parents who continue to put pressure on even after trying to talk about it. Emphasize that God has the power to get us through these pressures, but that they are not God's perfect will for us; they are part of living in this imperfect world. Repeat the value of God's power.]

Your Response to Pressure

Your contentment in the midst of pressure is largely determined by the way you react to it. Pressure is here to stay; it won't go away. Hopefully your parents help you handle the pressures in your life rather than make them worse. But even if your primary source of negative pressure is your parents, you can choose to respond in ways that help you achieve and grow a balanced life. You can choose the types of pressure you yield to. You can make it through destructive pressures and thrive under creative ones.

What's good and bad about each of these reactions to pressure?

	Good	*Bad*
Let pressure roll off like water off a duck's back.		
Handle pressure one step at a time like a turtle.		
Hibernate from pressure like a bear.		
Soar above pressure like an eagle.		

	Good	*Bad*
Have fun in the midst of pressure like a puppy.		
Swim through pressure like a fish.		
_____ pressure like a _____.		

If you were creating an animal that reacts to pressure in God's ideal way, what would it be like? What features from what animals would you combine and why? Don't limit yourself to the above examples. Feel free to add Bible verses to support your answer. Describe or draw the animal here.

How are you like this animal? How can you become more like it?

 BODYLIFE
Choose Positive Pressure
Parental and family pressure can be good or bad or a combination of both. Recall that creative pressure helps you solve a problem, accomplish a goal, keep going, or stop bad pressure. Destructive pressure makes you doubt yourself and your God-given goodness, threatens to stop good pressure. Rank each of the following pressure situations on a scale from 1-10 with 10 being creative pressure and 1 being destructive pressure. Then under each pressure write good things the creative pressure brings. Under each destructive pressure, write ways to ease the pressure or to make the pressure creative.

WHAT'S A KID LIKE ME DOING IN A FAMILY LIKE THIS?

	DESTRUCTIVE PRESSURE							CREATIVE PRESSURE		
	1	2	3	4	5	6	7	8	9	10

Hillary's mom insists she finish her homework before watching TV or going out with friends.

Harry's mom wants him to be valedictorian and grumbles about anything less than a perfect grade.

Hannie's dad wants her to do her best in gymnastics. He attends her meets, congratulates her successes, and assures her she'll do better next time on her fumbles.

Hal's dad wants him to be the first-string quarterback on the football team. He is satisfied with nothing less.

Hilda's parents encourage her to join others at church for worship, Bible study, and fellow-

	DESTRUCTIVE PRESSURE							CREATIVE PRESSURE		
	1	2	3	4	5	6	7	8	9	10

ship. They suggest she go about twice a week. They place an even higher priority on the way she lives for Christ from day to day.

Ho's parents insist that he and they be at the church building every time the door is opened. Ho gets the impression that attending church services and activities is the way to be spiritual.

☞ **[HELP: The first statement of every pair is more creative while the second one is more destructive. Invite group members to tell the reasons for their choices, noting that the details they add determine the nature of the pressure. The stories are written generally for this purpose. Ask: When are pressures both creative and destructive? How can a destructive pressure become creative? How do you pressure your family in destructive ways? Creative ways?]**

Life Response

Part of the problem with parental pressure is expecting different things. Parents who push you to be valedictorian might not realize that you want to be an excellent learner but don't want to drive yourself crazy by striving for the top. The two of you agree that you both want excellence in school. By focusing on these similarities, you can turn destructive pressure into creative pressure.

Write your expectations in the following areas. Invite your parents to do the same on separate paper. Then together pinpoint similarities and identify ways to focus on them.

	What I want	What my parents seem to want	What we both want
SCHOOL			
CHURCH			
SPIRITUALITY			
FRIENDSHIP			
JOB			
DATING			
FAMILY			
SPORTS			
TIME			
COMPETITION			
OTHER:			

☞ [HINT: Guide group members to write what they expect during class and talk with their parents about what they expect at home. Or suggest they write what they think their parents expect and note similarities during the session. They can then repeat the process at home to find out what their parents really think. Guide the group to encourage each other rather than to compare home horror stories.]

☞ [HELP: These Additional Life Responses are included in the group member book to allow them to choose a way to follow through. Challenge members to check one to do at home.]

Additional Life Responses
Check one or more to do at home.

1. Write separate letters to both parents, thanking them for ways they help you through outside pressures. Thank them also for specific pressures they put on you that "cook" you into a happier and more loving person. (Recall the pressure cooker.)

2. Write a prayer, talking with God about how He has or could help you through the pressures in your life. Notice that God helps you both by guiding your parents to place certain creative pressures on you and by helping you to manage parental pressures He didn't choose.

3. Play Amy Grant's "How Can We See That Far" on *Heart in Motion* (Myrrh, 1991). Then answer this question: How can the way we react to destructive pressures change them to creative pressures?

What's Next?
"Why Can't My Parents Understand?" — Do you have more trouble understanding your parents, or do your parents have more trouble understanding you?

THREE

▼

Why Can't My Parents Understand?

SESSION OVERVIEW

Purpose:
This session focuses on skills for mutual understanding that can equip group members to grow a closeness with parents that produces happiness at home.

Needs:
A primary complaint of adolescents is, "My parents don't understand!"

This statement can mean:
- My parents won't listen.
- I can't say what I really think and feel.
- They won't accept what I really think and feel.
- My parents won't let me do what I want to do.
- My parents want me to be like someone else.
- I don't understand my parents.
- We don't agree.

When young people crave understanding, they want not just clarity but to be heard, to be able to talk honestly and be accepted, to have some freedom to choose, to be loved for who they are, to experience mutuality.

Goals:
The goals for the *leader* include
(1) guiding members through simulated misunderstanding so they will more vigorously study its solutions;
(2) guiding members to experience understanding in the group so they will more energetically grow it at home;
(3) encouraging participants to name specific ways to obey several Bible tips on understanding;
(4) equipping group members to deliberately understand their family members.

The goals for the *group members* are that they will
(1) pinpoint an understanding need in their own homes;
(2) name ways to obey Bible tips on understanding;
(3) practice the understanding process of listening, noting initial reactions, and responding in a God-honoring way.

Life Response:
Group members will discover that their need for loving communication is not that much different from their parents'. They will pinpoint ways to become more lovingly honest with their parents and invite the same honesty in return.

Resource Materials:
___ Bibles
___ pens or pencils
___ one copy of *What's a Kid Like Me Doing in a Family Like This?* (student book) for each group member
___ bandages
___ a bag of chocolates

Pacing
See time suggestions in Session 2.

♥ HEARTBEAT

As group members enter, divide them into two groups on opposite sides of the room and direct them to share concerns and praises. When all have arrived, privately give one group bandages and promise each member one chocolate for every bandage the group can attach to another person. Privately offer the other group one chocolate per member for every bandage they take off a person. Bring groups together and start. After two minutes, count bandages on and off.

Ask: How do you feel? Why? Note feelings of frustration and success. Did you tell each other why you were acting differently? What you were working for? Why or why not?

Point out that both groups were working for chocolate but trying to get it in opposite ways. Award chocolates. Ask:

- What difference did it make, or would it have made, if you had told each other how you were able to get chocolate?
- Why was understanding the key to solving your frustration? How could understanding have helped you both get what you wanted?
- Compare this activity to understanding in your home. When do you and your parents work for the same thing in different ways? (Examples include: happiness, love, friendship.) How might understanding help you achieve what you both want?

Encourage group members to identify the specific understanding issues in their homes by completing the first section in their books.

Understanding at My House

Understanding is the key to building harmony, solving conflicts, and growing family closeness. What is the num-

ber one understanding need in your house? Mark it with a U. How do you understand each other well? Check all the statements that apply.
- [ ] To be heard.
- [ ] To talk honestly.
- [ ] To accept each other even when we disagree.
- [ ] To have some freedom to choose.
- [ ] To be loved for who we are.
- [ ] To feel the same about things that matter.
- [ ] To make choices we both agree with.
- [ ] _____

How do you know when you don't have understanding? Check all that apply. Circle the one you feel most strongly about.
- [ ] My parents won't listen.
- [ ] I can't say what I really think and feel.
- [ ] They won't accept what I really think and feel.
- [ ] My parents want me to be like someone else.
- [ ] My parents don't like my ideas or plans.
- [ ] I don't understand my parents.
- [ ] We don't agree.
- [ ] _____

How would your parents answer the same two questions?

☞ **[HINT: Invite group members to share reasons for choices and good examples of understanding along with the bad. Encourage the group to show compassion for frustration and congratulations for success. Note that not liking an idea is not always misunderstanding; it may be protection or care.]**

☞ **[HELP: Transition to the next section with optimism. Too many assume family understanding is impossible. It is not only possible but preferable. Assure members that our need for understanding is important to God** and He can help us grow understanding at home. Agree that He does His best work when all family members cooperate with Him but He can also work with one member at a time. Explore ways to let Him do this.]

LIFELINE
Tips for Talk that Understands

God knows of your desire for understanding, and this desire is important to Him. It is so important that He has given you guidance for achieving it. You'll find understanding tips scattered throughout the Bible. We'll sample some in James, Timothy, John, Proverbs, and Mark.

Find in James 1:19-26 the verse that gives each of the following tongue tips. Then name ways to use each tip to grow understanding in your family.

Verse	Tip	Way my family uses/ could use the tip
_____	Be quick to listen.	
_____	Be slow to speak.	
_____	Be slow to become angry.	
_____	Get rid of all moral filth.	
_____	Humbly accept the Word of God.	
_____	Do what God's Word says.	
_____	Don't forget what God says.	
_____	Keep a tight rein on your tongue.	

Now delve into the meaning of these tongue tips by exploring the following questions with your group. As you explore, add more ideas to the third column.

☞ [HINT: The goals of this section are Bible searching, honest sharing, receptive listening, and supportive caring. Suggest that each group member choose one communication issue to comment on. Doing so allows them to explore the issues that most affect them and encourages everyone to talk.]

What does listening have to do with understanding? Why does being quick to listen (v. 19) improve communication? Show love?

Some family members don't talk enough. How does being "slow to speak" (v. 19) apply to them?

Anger is not bad, but some expressions of anger are (v. 19). Conversely, holding anger in does not work because anger held in becomes depression. How might you let your anger out in slow and caring ways rather than explosive and destructive ways?

☞ [HELP: Explain that anger is a warning sign that something is wrong. It is not an end in itself. Discovering what's wrong is the key to expressing anger. For example, if you get angry every time someone disagrees with you, you can become slow to anger by seeing the good in another's point. If you become angry when your parents forbid something, you can work together to agree on what is permissible and why.]

James 1:20 says human anger does not bring about the life God desires. Is it possible for people to feel and express godly anger? How might you transform your anger energy into understanding energy?

Second Timothy 3:1-5 lists examples of moral filth James mentioned (v. 21). Which actions or attitudes are you most guilty of? Because your actions are the only ones you can control, how will you clean up your act? How might you invite family members to do the same? How does God want you to respond if they don't?

WHAT'S A KID LIKE ME DOING IN A FAMILY LIKE THIS?

Why is it easier to talk about God's Word than to do it (vv. 22-25)? Share an example from your life.

On a scale of 1-10, how easy is it for you to control your tongue (v. 26)?

☞ [HELP: Explain that rather than restrain the horse, a tight rein helps the horse perform well. Ask: How does control bring freedom rather than constraint?]

Tips for Tone that Understands

Understanding is more than just saying what you think and hearing what others think. It's doing so with compassion and sensitivity. Understanding accepts and loves even in disagreement. Understanding lets love lead to deeper understanding. Match these understanding principles to samples of how to do them.

___ 1. "Stop judging by mere appearances, and make a right judgment" (John 7:24).

a. Timing has a lot to do with clear communication. Example: Don't talk with your dad about buying new shoes the same day he loses his job.

___ 2. "A gentle answer turns away wrath, but a harsh word stirs up anger" (Proverbs 15:1).

b. Tell what you think you see, rather than accuse a family member of a certain attitude or action. The family member can then confirm or clarify your perception. Doing so keeps defensiveness down. Example: "I feel like you're not listening to what I say" rather than "You never listen to anything I say."

___ 3. "If a man loudly blesses his neighbor early in the morning, it will be taken as a curse" (Proverbs 27:14).

c. You can make a situation better or worse by the words you respond with. Example: When your parents yells at you, listen calmly rather than yell back.

___ 4. "A quarrelsome wife is like a constant dripping on a rainy day" (Proverbs 27:15).

d. Your attitude impacts how people feel about talking to you. Example: If you want to see or start problems, you'll find them. If you want to solve problems, you will.

___ 5. "Love your neighbor as yourself" (Mark 12:31).

e. An understanding tone boils down to being considerate. Treat your parents with the understanding actions you want. Example: If you want your parents to treat you with respect, show respect to them.

☞ [HELP: Planned matches are 1-b, 2-c, 3-a, 4-d, 5-e. But consider the wisdom of other matches group members choose. Invite members to share other communication tips from their own favorite Bible verses.]

BODYLIFE
Practice for Real Life Understanding
Use your understanding tips from the LIFELINE section to understand and respond to your family members. Understanding is ultimately a choice. Decide to understand your family members by taking steps to do so. Try this pattern:

WHAT'S A KID LIKE ME DOING IN A FAMILY LIKE THIS?

> Listen ➠ Note my initial response without speaking. ➠ Change my response to God's response. Then speak.

Practice on the following examples; the first one is completed. Then add one of your own.

What I heard	*My initial response*	*My expressed response*
After I'd been sick all weekend with the stomach flu, my mom said, "You're still going to make supper tonight, aren't you?"	I was hurt that she cared more about her fancy supper than my renewed health. I wanted to call my mom a selfish, uncaring pig.	I remembered I always cook on Mondays, and Mom looks forward to it every week. I said I'd be glad to cook but would do it Tuesday.
I asked to use the car, and Dad said I had to mow the lawn and clean my room first.		
My parents said I could attend the prom, but a limousine is too extravagant.		
My example:		

Understand to Bring Out Honesty

Understanding becomes complicated when people don't say exactly what they mean. Unfortunately, honesty and understanding work in a cycle:

If we understand and are understood, ➠ we tend to be honest ➠ which deepens understanding.

but

44

WHY CAN'T MY PARENTS UNDERSTAND?

| If we don't understand and aren't understood, ⇒ | we tend to say what we think others want to hear ⇒ | which keeps us from being understood, which keeps us from being honest. |

Why do we find it hard to be totally honest even in the beginning? Add your own idea; then rank these in order of occurrence.
- ☐ To look good
- ☐ To cover a problem
- ☐ Fear my idea will be rejected
- ☐ Selfish instead of other-centered
- ☐ Dishonesty worked in the past
- ☐ Don't know how to say what I want to say
- ☐ Other: _____

☞ **[HINT: Point out the love and understanding that happens in the group. Ask: How did we grow this love? How might the same actions grow understanding closeness in your family?]**

Write about a time you said more than you wanted to say, less than you wanted to say, or different words than you wanted to say. Why were you less than honest?

Tell about a time a family member did the same thing, or seemed to do so. Why do you think your family member was less than honest?

What words or actions might help both of you feel free to say what you need to say?

☞ **[HELP: Supplement with comments like these: Obviously, the key is to say what you mean and mean what you say. At the same time, we need to receive honest communication even when we don't like it. To do so, listen carefully and compassionately to family mem-**

bers. Then tell them what you hear and invite them to correct any misperceptions. Invite them to help you understand.]

Life Response

As you and your parent(s) understand each other's thoughts, feelings, strengths, and weaknesses, you can grow the kind of closeness you both crave. As you understand each other's goals and ways you work toward those goals, you can make decisions together and discover actions that give you both what you want. To practice accepting the honesty and understanding your parents might offer you, think about these sample statements. When might you say them to a parent? When might your parent(s) say them to you? What might God want you to do about both?

☞ [HINT: Especially if time is short, share ideas in cell groups of two or three members. This allows time for more people to do more sharing.]

	I say it when	My parent says it when	God wants me to
"You embarrass me when you _____."			
"You never listen to me. All I have to do is mention _____ and you launch into lecture mode."			
"Just leave me alone!"			
"Why can't you understand how important this is?"			
Other: _____			

Many understanding problems can be solved simply by treating your parents the way you want to be treated (Mark 12:28-31). When you want understanding or respect

WHY CAN'T MY PARENTS UNDERSTAND?

or consideration, give it to your parents. What specific words and actions will you use to give these?

How will you invite communication, respect, and consideration from your parents?

> **Close by calling on a volunteer to read Mark 12:28-31, emphasizing verse 31. Explain that increasing the quality of communication is a way to obey God.**

☞ **[HELP: Additional Life Responses. Use the first one in the group meeting, and suggest the others for follow-through at home:
1. Invite group members to read or tell about the letter, prayer, or song that came while completing the Additional Life Response for Session 2. Affirm each.
2. Evaluate what you read and watch this week to discover truths about understanding. What makes it happen? What destroys it?
3. Consider what might happen if you treated your parents like friends and your friends like parents.
4. Ask a volunteer to read and share a few excerpts from *Sometimes I Really Hate You!* by Dewey Bertolini (Victor Books). Suggest an excerpt that relates to communication (today's session) and one that relates to security (next week's topic).]**

What's Next?

"Give Me Roots So I Can Fly" — What security do you need from your parents to be truly independent?

FOUR

▼

Give Me Roots So I Can Fly

SESSION OVERVIEW

Purpose:
This session guides group members to explore how their parents' care gives them the security they need to grow toward independence.

Needs:
Contrary to appearances, adolescents still yearn for closeness with their parents. But because the closeness they need is now different, both parents and teens often assume they don't need each other. They actually need each other more, especially for encouragement, interest, and guidance.

Sadly, some parents can't or won't give the security and support their teens need.

Expressions of love are not easy for young people or their parents. Teens may express their frustration with rebellion or apathy. Parents may express their frustration by clamping down or by letting go too rapidly. As parents, adolescents, and God work together, they can turn frustration into a healthy journey toward independence.

Because God is the ultimate source of security, He will

provide it in both caring and uncaring home situations. Parents are important vehicles of God-given security, but they are not the only ones. He will use other vehicles if parents don't fulfill their God-given parenting obligations.

Goals:
The goals for the *leader* include
(1) creating opportunity for members to affirm one another;
(2) guiding members to share the need for a secure home;
(3) recognizing God as the One who gives security through parents or independent from parents;
(4) encouraging group members to take responsibility for enriching their part of home relationships.

The goals for the *group members* are that they will
(1) recognize that it's OK to still need parents and home;
(2) embrace God as the ultimate source of security;
(3) notice what they need and how God can meet their needs.

Life Response:
Group members will practice asking parents for what they need and thank them for what they have given.

Resource Materials:
___ Bibles
___ pens or pencils
___ one copy of *What's a Kid Like Me Doing in a Family Like This?* (student book) for each group member
___ agree/disagree signs and masking tape

Pacing:
See time suggestions in Session 2.

♥ HEARTBEAT

Half Time

You're now halfway through this study of family relationships. Reaffirm your covenant with the others in your group. Write their names below and what you appreciate about each or something she or he has taught you about loving at home.

Name   Why I appreciate you/what you've taught me

Share your appreciation with these persons. Thank God for your family of brothers and sisters in Christ.

☞ [HINT: Stand behind each member, and invite the group to tell why they're glad this person is in the group and what he or she has taught them about family. Then invite volunteers to share how they have cared differently in their families as a result of this group. Guide a prayer of thankfulness for these brothers and sisters in Christ. Give a group hug.]

Home Base

As an emerging adult, you want freedom and independence; but you still need your parents. How are your needs for your parents different now? How do you need them the same as you used to need them? What new expressions of care do you need?

☞ [HINT: Post AGREE, DISAGREE, STRONGLY AGREE, STRONGLY DISAGREE signs on four walls and invite group members to move to the sign that tells how they feel. As they explain their reasons, they bring out the many facets of the security/freedom issue. Emphasize that each situation and detail they say can highlight an aspect of the truth.]

GIVE ME ROOTS SO I CAN FLY

SA = Strongly Agree   A = Agree   D = Disagree
SD = Strongly Disagree

SA A D SD   1. Now that I'm an emerging adult, I still need my parents' love to give me security.

☞ [HELP: Invite group members to suggest actions from parents that give security such as interest, empathy, mutually-set rules, advice, acceptance, encouragement to live for Christ.]

SA A D SD   2. Independence means I don't need anyone.

☞ [HELP: Include the What's Next? question from last week. Ask: How do roots give you wings? How do wings give roots?]

SA A D SD   3. I still want hugs and other physical expressions of care from my parents.
SA A D SD   4. I still want advice but want it in a new way.
SA A D SD   5. My parents love me like I want to be loved.

☞ [HELP: For statements 3–5, suggest sharing a way group members do and don't.]

SA A D SD   6. My parents balance guidance with freedom.

☞ [HELP: Notice frustrations on both ends of the spectrum: "They won't let me decide for myself!" vs. "They don't care what I do anymore." Invite members to identify ways to ask for balance.]

SA   A   D   SD   7. I need my parents to give me a home and a foundation by _____.

☞ **[HELP: Ask group members to tell how they completed this statement. During LIFELINE, guide group members to cite specific actions that can turn rebellious feelings into a healthy quest for independence.]**

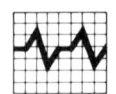

LIFELINE
Run the Bases

We want and need a home base of security and can-count-on-it love from our parents. God knows about this need since He created it. Parents serve as primary imparters of the confidence that gives us the abilities to succeed in relationships, school, work, and faith expression. Keeping in mind that no parent is perfect, name parental actions through which God gave you security at these ages.

☞ **[HINT: Remind group members that parent means the adult(s) you live with.]**

INFANCY:

PRESCHOOL:

ELEMENTARY SCHOOL:

MIDDLE SCHOOL/HIGH SCHOOL:

NOW:

☞ **[HELP: Point out the ball game theme of this session in the heads. Suggest that giving security is not a one-time action but a series of actions that helps you enjoy participating in the game of life. Ask: When have your parents hit homers? When did they strike out? Bunt? Walk? How does your attitude as a player impact how well your parents equip you?]**

GIVE ME ROOTS SO I CAN FLY

Read 1 Corinthians 13:11-12. These verses explain that we've come a long way since childhood and we now have a long way to go. As we learn about God, people, and life, we need our parents to help us along.

Identify a way your parents help you move toward maturity:

Identify another way you wish they would help:

God understands both the gratefulness and frustration you feel over your parents. He knows parents and home are important. In fact, His commandment about parents is the first one with a promise: "Honor your father and your mother, as the Lord your God has commanded you, so that you may live long and that it may go well with you in the land the Lord your God is giving you" (Deuteronomy 5:16).

Your response to your parent(s) impacts how well your parent can love you. Circle your favorite synonym for honor.

Value	Show respect for	Esteem
Cherish	Give credit to	Admire
Accept	Be honest with	Your idea: _____

☞ **[HELP: A synonym is a word that means the same as another word.]**

Obviously, it's not all up to you. Your parents must try too. But family closeness is a two-way street. How does honoring your parents make it possible for them to give you the security and support you need?

How does honoring give you a long and happy life?

WHAT'S A KID LIKE ME DOING IN A FAMILY LIKE THIS?

☞ [HELP: Living long is not always measured chronologically. It is also a quality of life, a depth and "intouchness."]

How does honoring help things go better for you?

Parents (and teens) lose some of their God-given honor when they disobey God. How do you think God wants you to respond when your parents don't deserve honor? When they don't give you the parenting you need? Why?

Turn to the Coach for Pinch Hitters
In families, like in a ball game, everyone has a part to play. But sometimes parents won't do their part. God then steps in with a pinch hitter or two. If your parents aren't around, treat you poorly, or have given you no security except life itself, God can still give you a secure foundation. He usually uses parents to give you this home base, but when they can't or won't give it, He'll use a grandparent, an adult at church, or a series of other people.

Choose an item in the room that illustrates how it feels when your parents fail you. Tell why.

☞ [HELP: A concrete image helps people express feelings. A group member might say, "I feel thrown against the wall when my mom criticizes me." Or, "My parents are like a window that helps me see the truth." Or, "I feel like the smelly trash in that basket when my dad ignores me."]

Choose an item that illustrates how it feels when your parents give you security. Tell why.

Whether your parents care or not, name another adult God has used to love you. How does this person care?

God's steady and personal love is the constant in your life.

How is God your source of security when your parents fail you? When they give you a secure home?

God promises this kind of security only to those who are His children through faith in Jesus Christ and who submit to Him as Lord. If you have not trusted Him, see Romans 10:9-11 and 12:1-2 for the necessary steps.

☞ [HINT: Invite volunteers to share why they are Christians and how their faith gives them foundation and security.]

☞ [HINT: Focus most of your LIFELINE time on this next section. It most directly conveys the central focus of the session.]

Learn from the Coach

Deepen your certainty of your God-given worth and security by identifying ways these truths occur in your life.

Philippians 4:12-13: I have been in need of _____

when _____.

I have had plenty of _____ when _____.

God enabled me to be content by _____

_____.

Philippians 4:19: God has met my need for _____

by _____.

Revelation 21:3b-4: I know God is with me because ____

_____.

He wipes my tears away by _____

_____.

☞ **[HELP: Invite group members to share other favorite Bible verses and how God gives them security through these promises.]**

☞ **[HELP: Assure group members that God knows about and cares about our family pleasure and family pain. He rejoices when things go well. He cries along with us and is sad when our families aren't loving. Just as deeply as He feels our pain, He works with us to redeem that pain and to give us the secure foundation we need.]**

BODYLIFE
How I Win the Game

Security with God is real whether we feel it or not. How can we feel and believe this security? You and fellow group members can convince yourselves by reading Bible promises, and by reminding one another of your foundation in Christ. Name a way you'll increase the security of a group member.

Affirm the way God works to give you home-like security by writing a story about it. If your parents love you well, notice. If they don't love you in all ways, notice how they do love you. If your parents don't love you now in the way you need to be loved, notice ways they may have loved you in the past. If they didn't love you well as a child, notice ways they love you now. Some parents do better with one age group than another. Tell your own security story. For example:

My parents were great when I was little, giving me

their presence, playing games in the yard, taking me to scouts and more. When I began thinking for myself, they withdrew from me, criticized me, and attacked my ideas. They could relate to me as a child but not as an independently thinking young adult. When people learn of my parents' steady rejection from adolescence on, they wonder why I survived. I think it was the bit of security my folks gave during my early days and my relationship with my grandfather who did accept me and my ideas. These measures of God's grace gave me a foundation.

Your security story:

☞ [HINT: While group members tell their stories, reinforce active listening, compassion, and affirmation. Point out care from the body of Christ as a way God imparts security. Consider sharing in pairs if time is short.]

Life Response: Asking Practice

Part of growing an adult relationship is asking for what you need. Because parents can't read your mind to know what kind of loving you want, tell them. This is communication. It is also building a mature relationship. As a young child, your parents anticipated your needs and met them. Now you must take more responsibility for letting them know what you want and need. You'll use the same skill in marriage.

Begin by pinpointing what you want. What is home? What do you need it to be? Many say home is the place where you belong and can be yourself. Others call home a haven from the cruel world. Still others say home is the place you go to for help, support, and advice and is the place you give these same qualities to other family members. If you could transform your family into the perfect home, what three wishes would you make?

WISH #1:

WISH #2:

WISH #3:

Wishes seldom come true by just wishing. Wishes come true by working toward them and by asking your parents for what you need. Practice by trading wishes with another group member and writing a letter asking for these wishes. Base your advice on Bible passages and your experience as a Christian. The following examples can help you know how to write your wishes. Notice they are specific rather than "I want Mom to love me."

> I WISH FOR HONESTY. Michelle's mom is not big on reality. When Michelle remained small-chested long after puberty, her mom kept insisting her breasts would grow. Michelle knew that was all talk. She wished her mother would point out the beauty in the body Michelle had rather than pretend she'd get another. How could Michelle ask for this without her mother denying it?

> I WISH YOU WOULD NOT PANIC. Jason has questions about God and how His principles apply to daily life. Every time Jason asks, "How do we know Christianity is the one way to God?" or "Does God really expect us to obey in every area?" his dad panics. "Don't doubt God!" or "Because the Bible says so!" he replies. Jason wishes his dad would help him understand specifics rather than make blanket statements. He wishes his dad would help him see what's unique about Jesus and how God's ways work. Jason wants to grow his faith, not just name it.

> I WISH TO BE ACCEPTED FOR WHO I AM. Kim has a

brilliant younger sister who is glamorous, school smart, and enjoys the same things as her mom. Kim is simple in beauty, sports smart, and likes different things than her mom. She feels her dad likes her sister better. She wants him to hear and understand her ideas and goals. She wants him to see her beauty. How can she ask without sounding competitive?

Life Response: Appreciation Practice
Perhaps your parents give you some or all of the security you need to become independent. What do you like about what they do? What would you have a hard time living without? Write your parent(s) a letter of thanks for the ways he or she loves you. Next to the letter, draw a trophy you'd give him or her.

Close by reading Ephesians 3:16-19, emphasizing verse 17.

☞ [HELP: Additional Life Responses to include if time allows or to suggest for follow-through at home:
1. Ask the enlisted volunteer to share a few excerpts from *Sometimes I Really Hate You!* by Dewey Bertolini. Invite group members to share ways they have overcome bitterness.
2. Create a visual about roots and wings, perhaps basing it on Ephesians 3:16-19, especially verse 17.
3. Ask: How will you create a home when you are a parent? Write yourself a letter including these commitments.]

What's Next?
"They Love Her More Than Me" — How well do each of your parent(s) know, understand, and accept you? How well do you know, understand, and accept them?

FIVE

▼

They Love Her More Than Me

SESSION OVERVIEW

Purpose:
This session provides strategies for loving each family member as a unique and valuable part of the family.

Needs:
A major complaint in families with more than one child is, "They love her more than they love me!" Because even children raised in the same family have different personalities and temperaments, parents tend to treat children differently. Doing so is not always bad. Different treatment becomes bad when parents favor one child. This can lead to genuine unfairness. (See Genesis 27:5-13.)

A second complaint is, "He's impossible to live with! This session encourages group members to view each family member as a valuable person.

As adolescents learn to accept other family members, they need acceptance from their parents. Although they cannot control their parents' behavior, they can invite fair and loving treatment. They can help parents see their strengths. Conversely, adolescents must treat parents with the individual love they want from them. Too often adolescents want their parents to love them for who they are but refuse to accept the personalities and unique gifts of their parents.

Acceptance is a complex issue. It requires accepting different personalities, inviting change for wrong behaviors, and distinguishing between the two. This session guides group members to explore the acceptance issue. As adolescents give their parents the respect and acceptance they want from them, they can grow truly loving relationships.

Goals:

The goals for the *leader* include
(1) creating appreciation for both siblings and parents;
(2) illustrating why each family member is important;
(3) guiding group members to distinguish between healthy and need-to-be-changed differences;
(4) motivating acceptance of parents and siblings.

The goals for the *group members* are that they will
(1) identify characteristics they value in their siblings;
(2) discover why differences are important;
(3) ask family members to accept them as individuals;
(4) accept other family members as individuals.

Life Response:

Recalling that they themselves don't want to be pressed into a certain mold, group members will refuse to insist their parents fit a preset mold.

Resource Materials:

— Bibles and pens or pencils
— one copy of *What's a Kid Like Me Doing in a Family Like This?* (student book) for each group member
— clay or other shaping material (optional)

Pacing:

See time suggestions in Session 2.

♥ HEARTBEAT
Sibling Saga

Living with sisters, brothers, stepsisters, and stepbrothers has both delightful and dreaded elements. One of the dreaded elements is when your parents favor one sibling over you. The way you relate to both siblings and parents can minimize or eliminate this favoritism. You cannot choose how your parents treat you or your siblings, but you can invite fair treatment. You can also treat your siblings and parents with the same respect you want from them. Begin by pinpointing needs. Check all that apply in each column.

What do you like about living with siblings?	*What bothers you about living with siblings?*
☐ Company	☐ No privacy
☐ Someone who understands	☐ Wants me to see his/her side
☐ We're good friends	☐ Irritate each other
☐ Game partner	☐ Wants to do everything I do
☐ Always available	☐ Always around
☐ Can share wardrobe	☐ Borrows my clothes without asking
☐ Gives me advice	☐ Always tells me what to do
☐ My parents like us both	☐ My parents like him/her better
☐ _____	☐ _____

How would your sibling(s) fill out the chart about you? Put an S next to the boxes for each sibling's response. Where do they feel the same as you? Differently?

Your sibling may want to be with you more than you want

to be with him or her. You may like to do things both similarly and differently than your sibling. Either of you may get mad at the other even though you love each other. How do you manage your opposite needs?

> [HELP: Present these opposites as two sides of the same coin. Even those who love each other need privacy, etc. Encourage group members to find ways to meet opposite needs through such actions as talking through anger and giving each other a balance of together time and privacy.]

Can your parents treat you and your sibling(s) differently and still be fair? Give examples of a "yes" and "no" answer.

> [HELP: Yes: A younger child needs more guidance than an older one. No: All children need their parents' love and support.]

YES:

NO:

When is different treatment actually fair treatment? How would loving the same way take away your individuality?

> [HELP: Suggest an example like this one: You are older and come in on time so you can stay out later than a younger sibling who breaks curfew.]

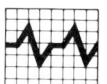

LIFELINE
It All Depends on What You Do with It
Any time you live with more than one person, there will be problems to overcome. These conflicts and problems come not because either of you is bad but because of natural personality differences and preferences.

WHAT'S A KID LIKE ME DOING IN A FAMILY LIKE THIS?

Differences can weave together to create the beautiful tapestry called family, or they can create continual discord and strife. *When the love of Christ predominates, you can find the unity you want in your family.*

Recalling the needs you identified at the beginning of this session, search Romans 12:9-21 for specific actions that will show the love of Christ in the midst of conflicting needs. Work with a partner to list at least ten.

1. 6.
2. 7.
3. 8.
4. 9.
5. 10.

Now choose a shows-the-love-of-Christ action and identify a specific sentence or deed that would show you were living this action in your family.

☞ **[HELP: Example for "honor one another above yourselves" (v. 10): I'll share the car rather than insisting on having it all the time. Example for "overcome evil with good" (v. 21): When my sister yells at me, I'll respond calmly rather than attacking her with worse accusations.]**

☞ **[HINT: Point out indicators of the closeness in the group, such as interest, sharing, comfort. Ask: How do we accept diversity and treat each other fairly here in the group? How could the same actions transfer to home?]**

Unity in Diversity

God's Word has plenty to say about getting along in groups. One of the most important groups you'll ever be part of is your family. Read 1 Corinthians 12:12-27 in the light of your family. Then write at least three phrases from these verses that describe your family.

1.
2.
3.

Note specific ways you might apply the following phrases in your family.

Bible phrase   *How we can live it at home*

Though all its parts are many, they form one body (v. 12).

If the foot should say, "Because I am not a hand, I do not belong to the body," it would not for that reason cease to be part of the body (v. 15).

☞ [HELP: Encourage group members to help everyone in their families feel they belong and are important. Ask: How could you do so? Add ideas like: You may not be like your sibling, but you are just as important in your family. Each is important whether they or we feel like they are.]

If the whole body were an eye, where would the sense of hearing be? If the whole body were an ear, where would the sense of smell be? (v. 17).

☞ [HELP: No one family member can do all the loving or caring the family needs. Invite group members to suggest in cell groups of two or three persons the contributions each family member makes in his or her family. Ask: What is unique and important about each contribution?]

But in fact God has arranged
the parts in the body, every
one of them, just as He
wanted them to be (v. 18).

☞ [HELP: Ask: What is God's will for your family? Explain that everything that happens in families is not God's will because people may work against His will. God wants family members to appreciate each other, care for each other, and guide each other to grow. When members refuse to do this, God is not pleased. Ask: How can you obey God no matter how other family members act?]

The eye cannot say to the
hand, "I don't need you!"
And the head cannot say to
the feet, "I don't need you!"
(v. 21).

☞ [HELP: We can't make it on our own. We need our families and our families need us. What problems are caused when we refuse to be there for each other? To admit our needs?]

There should be no division
in the body, but that its parts
should have equal concern
for each other (v. 25).

☞ [HINT: Some group members will have tremendous division in their families, either obvious ones of divorce and separation or hidden divisions called silent treatment, grudges, rejection, and favoritism. Show sensitivity, and encourage group members to do the same. Point out similar feelings experienced in both intact and physically divided families. Suggest that if parents and other family members refuse to create unity, group members can learn unity-creating skills for their own future families. Comment from the student book introduction on pages 5 and 6.]

If one part suffers, every part
suffers with it (v. 26).

If one part is honored, every
part rejoices with it (v. 26).

☞ [HELP: Invite members to suggest sentences they can use to share suffering and honor with specific family members.]

Now you are the body of
Christ, and each one of you is
a part of it (v. 27).

☞ [HELP: Encourage group members to name ways the group creates the oneness described here. Ask: How can we use these same actions in our families?]

Family Portrait
Keeping 1 Corinthians 12:12-27 in mind, name a specific reason you need each person in your family. Include both those who live with you and those who live in other locations.

Name   Action, characteristic, or quality I need

Did you name actions, characteristics, and qualities different from or identical to you? How do differences enhance you? How do the similarities draw you close?

How does each family member do the following?
- Point out your strengths:
- Encourage you to improve weaknesses:
- Make you feel good about your God-given worth:
- Enjoy being with you:
- Bring out the best in you:
- Give you pleasure:

☞ [HINT: Note that some family members will do all of these, while some may do only one. Have group members share what they wrote in cells groups of two to four.]

How do you do the same for each family member?
- Point out strengths:
- Encourage the member to improve weaknesses:
- Make him or her feel good about God-given worth:
- Enjoy being with him or her:
- Bring out the best:
- Give pleasure:

Using the above ideas, draw a picture of your family as a body or other cooperating unit. What piece would you be? Each sibling? Each parent?

☞ [HINT: Encourage group members to use their creativity to create a visual of family unity and cooperation in the midst of diversity. Some will feel safer drawing a body. Others will choose their own forms. Affirm the wisdom in both by focusing on the placement of specific family members.]

BODYLIFE
Destruction in Diversity
We've studied God's ideal, but family members don't always cooperate with God. Your parent may expect you

to be just like a sibling in grades, personality, or other areas. This problem has caused pain since Jacob and Esau. (See Genesis 25:19-34; 27:1-41; 32:1–33:15.) Identify one or two pains you've seen it cause.

What solutions have you found for it? (Search Romans 12:9-21 and 1 Corinthians 12:12-27 for ideas.)

Sometimes siblings act cruelly or otherwise create pain in families. Identify one or two pains siblings—including yourself—have caused.

☞ **[HINT: Let this be a confession time as well as pain-sharing time. Minimize "us against them" feelings by asking the following questions.]**

What makes siblings (or you) act this way?

☞ **[HELP: Examples include power, defensiveness, insecurity, anger, threat.]**

What actions from Romans 12:9-21 or 1 Corinthians 12:12-27 could replace these cruel sibling actions?

Choose to Create Love
Whether your parents accept you or not, you can choose to value your parents. Whether your parents treat you and your siblings equally or not, you can choose to treat your parents well. Name a way you'll do so.

No matter how your parents treat your siblings and even if your siblings show little love for you, you can choose to show love for your siblings. Identify a specific sentence or action you'll use to do so.

How might you and your siblings find the willingness and ability to learn from each other rather than compete?

Life Response

You want to be accepted for who you are without being pressed into a mold set by your parents. Grant your parents the same favor. Refuse to insist that they fit your preset mold.

Draw or describe the mold you want your parent(s) to fit.

Parent #1:   *Parent #2 (step or other parent):*

☞ **[HINT: Consider letting group members shape perfect parents out of clay and then describe their creations. See the value of clay shaping in Session 1.]**

☞ **[HELP: Define parent as the adult or adults who care for you. This may be a biological or adoptive parent, a stepparent, a single parent, or a paired couple.]**

Get to know and accept your parents as they are. How do your parents differ from your mold? Is that OK? Why?

☞ **[HINT: Try Additional Life Response #2 here.]**

What healthy differences exist between you and your parents? How can you grow through them?

In cases of genuine wrongdoing, we have a right not to accept a parent's or a sibling's behavior. How can you communicate acceptance of the person as you reject a certain behavior?

How can you tell the difference between varying personalities and genuine wrong? When do you have a right to ask a family member to change?

☞ **[HELP: Example: A father abuses alcohol. Requesting he stop drinking is a legitimate request for change** since the drinking causes family strife, endangers lives, and harms her dad. Ask: How does God want us to respond when parents don't change? When destructive behavior continues?]

How might you invite your parent to know you, love you, accept you, and encourage you to grow?

When do your parents have a right to ask you to change?

☞ [HINT: Reduce defensiveness by recalling that we've just talked about asking parents to change and our motives were good ones. Then ask: What good motives might parents have to ask you to change? When their motives are not good ones, should you change? Why?]

Fit the Mold
What mold should we all try to fit according to Romans 12:1-2?

☞ [HELP: Emphasize that pleasing God and becoming like Christ are the guides for change. Many times parents urge this attitude and behavior without knowing it. Ask: Could God be working through your parents to grow you? Through you to grow them? How?]

How are families enhanced when we all work toward acting Christlike?

When one or two work toward it?

When you work toward it?

☞ [HINT: Motivate group members to take personal responsibility for their actions in their families rather than blaming someone else. Suggest focus on personal change rather than dwelling on others' strengths or shortcomings. Encourage them to commit to personal spiritual growth in specific ways.]

☞ [HELP: Additional Life Responses to include if time allows or to suggest for follow-through at home:

1. Play "Good For Me" from Amy Grant's *Heart in Motion* recording (Myrrh, 1991). Ask or think about: How do differences bring out the good in us? When do they cause more conflict than compassion? Note that moral differences are not mere matters of opinion; they cause division and damage.

2. Using separate sheets of paper for each, describe your parents and siblings. Include such items as favorite activities, life goals, something fun about him/her, what she/he likes thinking about, what makes him/her sad, what makes him/her happy, favorite memory, why she/he's a person of worth created in the image of God. (If you don't know about these things, ask!) Then close with a paragraph about why you like this family member and why you think he or she likes you. Consider giving a copy of this tribute to your family member in letter form.

3. Stage a "How Well Do You Know Your Parent?" game to encourage communication and acceptance among family members. Model it after a currently popular TV game show.]

What's Next?

"I'll Tell You What My Parents Think about God"—Do your parents enhance or frustrate your spiritual development? How and why? How can you become more spiritual in both circumstances?

SIX

▼

I'll Tell You What My Parents Think about God

SESSION OVERVIEW

Purpose:
This session guides participants to explore how their parents' commitment—or lack of commitment—to God impacts their faith expression. They will commit to being spiritual at home.

Needs:
Adolescents who are committed to Christ want and need encouragement to live their commitment. Some Christian adolescents have parents who enhance their spiritual obedience. Others have parents who frustrate it. In both cases, they can grow in Christ. Philippians 4:12-13 and Romans 8:28-39 explain that good times and bad times can enhance spiritual growth. As group members notice how well parents and other family members model Christianity, they'll discover examples they want to follow and others they want to refuse.

True spirituality shows itself in such daily experiences as family care, honesty, encouragement, conflict resolution, mutual goal setting, and respect. Many people connect spirituality with church going and Bible reading. These actions prepare us for spiritual living. They do not constitute it.

This session defines spirituality as doing what God says rather than acting in an other-worldly or out-of-touch way. Whether parents are uncommitted or deeply committed to God, adolescents can learn from and deepen their personal spiritual commitment in response.

Goals:
The goals for the *leader* include
(1) encouraging group members to take more responsibility for their part of family relationships;
(2) guiding group members to discern true spirituality;
(3) examining biblical passages on spiritual actions;
(4) creating an atmosphere of encouragement.

The goals for the *group members* are that they will
(1) define true spirituality;
(2) identify and commit to three specific actions that show spirituality;
(3) commit to grow in spiritual expression regardless of their home situations.

Life Response:
Whether their parents show no obedience to or deep obedience to God, group members will commit to deepening their personal spiritual obedience.

Resource Materials:
___ Bibles
___ pens or pencils
___ one copy of *What's a Kid Like Me Doing in a Family Like This?* (student book) for each group member

Pacing:
See time suggestions in Session 2.

♥ HEARTBEAT

Guide the group to examine true spirituality through the exaggerated answers in this quiz.

True Spirituality

Choose your favorite responses and tell why.

1. To be truly spiritual is to . . .
   a. live with your head in the clouds.
   b. say spiritual words like "holy," "Praise God," and "I love Jesus."
   c. obey Jesus in everyday life.
   d. be in touch with what matters: people, people's feelings, growth.

☞ [HELP: Explain that true spirituality is not otherworldliness (a) or holy talk (b), but day-to-day obedience and care (c, d). Agree that we are citizens of another kingdom (heaven) and that we should use Bible words, but we also obey God by being in touch and by showing faith in action.]

2. Truly spiritual people . . .
   a. wear holy clothes.
   b. say holy words.
   c. smile all the time.
   d. show their faith in their actions.

☞ [HELP: All the above can be correct but (d) encompasses them all. A Christian who shows faith in action wears clothes that honor God and aren't skimpy or showy. She chooses words that genuinely build people up rather than tear them down or sound fake. He shows honest emotion, conscious that weeping can be an expression of true Christian care. (See John 11:35-

36.) Options (a), (b), and (c) could be faked or substituted for true heart obedience.]

3. True spirituality . . .
   a. is very plain.
   b. says "no" to anything fun or interesting.
   c. is unromantic.
   d. is the most colorful, the most fun, the deepest, and the most interesting life available.
   e. grows the strongest friendships, marriages, and families because Christians learn how to love from the Creator of love, God Himself.

☞ [HELP: True spirituality is (d) and does (e). Some persons or groups have decided that true belief must be plain or boring, but this is not God's idea. Because Christians are in touch with the Creator, they are in touch with what matters and what gives joy. God teaches them how to grow the best friendships, marriages, schoolwork, and strongest families.]

4. Fake spirituality looks like . . .
   a. a plastic smile.
   b. someone who acts one way in church and totally different at school.
   c. someone who can say all the right answers but lives none of them.
   d. a wolf in lamb's clothing.
   e. _____ .

5. My favorite spiritual person is _____ because . . .
   a. she/he's sincere.
   b. she/he really cares.
   c. she/he shows faith by _____ .
   d. she/he understands the Bible and makes it clear.
   e. _____ .

I'LL TELL YOU WHAT MY PARENTS THINK ABOUT GOD

☞ **[HINT: Thinking of real people helps group members know how to be spiritual rather than just talk about it.]**

6. In my family, spirituality means . . .
   a. holding my tongue when I'm angry.
   b. being a peacemaker rather than making things worse.
   c. bringing out the good in other family members.
   d. being myself and appreciating the other selves in my family.
   e. _____.

☞ **[HELP: All can be correct. The right answer is the one that matches the group member. Encourage use of the blank space for more precise matches. Reemphasize spirituality as daily obedience in routine life.]**

During this session, commit to be spiritual in your family and pinpoint specific ways to do so. If you've not yet become a Christian, notice why Jesus is the one and only person who can give you security and family happiness.

☞ **[HINT: Compliment group members by pointing out that they are moving from blaming their parents to taking more responsibility for their part of family relationships. Affirm the maturity this action displays.]**

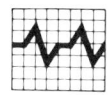

LIFELINE
Model for Spirituality

Jesus is our model for spirituality. He was tempted to sin, but He didn't do it (Matthew 4:1-11). His parents misunderstood Him, but He talked things over calmly with them (Luke 2:48-51). People around Him wanted Him to act in several different ways, but He chose God's ways.

Most of what we know about Jesus' life occurred before

age 2 and after age 30. His growing-up years are summarized in Luke 2:51-52. What do you think Jesus' growing up years were like? We know He learned from teachers in the synagogue. We assume He worked in the carpenter shop with His stepdad Joseph and brothers James, Joseph, Judas, and Simon (Mark 6:3). Do you think He complained about work? Did His sisters and brothers bug Him? Did congregational worship ever bore Him? How did He handle other real life experiences like relating to friends and to girls? What questions did He have, and how did He find answers? How was His life similar to and different from yours? Write or draw your impressions here.

☞ **[HELP: This section is built on speculation. Remind group members of this fact while at the same time encouraging them to identify with Jesus as a real person who followed God with no special privileges. Guide them to compare their ideas to the Bible. For example, Hebrews 2:17-18 and 4:14-16 explain that Jesus suffered when He was tempted and that He can help us.]**

Three Spiritual Actions
Pondering Jesus' life is helpful speculation. Bible passages like Micah 6:6-8 supplement that speculation with definite suggestions.

Read Micah 6:6-8. The actions Micah suggested in verses 6-7 were the religious actions of the time. The first several offerings had been recommended by God in similar form at one time or another. Child sacrifice was considered by some pagan groups to be the ultimate sacrifice, but God had never desired it (Jeremiah 19:5). What present religious actions do people call spiritual? What are the strengths and weaknesses of these?

What three actions has God commanded as evidence of

true spirituality according to Micah 6:8?
1.
2.
3.

Read these in several translations to discover the one you like best. Jot it down next to the above and cite the translation.

☞ [HELP: Sample translations include: NIV—"to act justly and to love mercy, and to walk humbly with your God"; KJV—"to do justly, and to love mercy, and to walk humbly with thy God"; NASB—"to do justice, to love kindness, and to walk humbly with your God"; LB—"to be fair and just and merciful, and to walk humbly with your God"; ICB—"Do what is right to other people. Love being kind to others. And live humbly, trusting your God."]

☞ [HINT: This section is designed to guide group members to study the Bible to discover who God is calling them to be. Guide them to find the truths for themselves instead of lecturing. Affirm biblical insight and specific ideas for applying the Bible as group members share them.]

True spirituality is doing what God says rather than acting in an other-worldly or out-of-touch way. It is faith in action. How will you obey the three Micah 6:8 actions in your home? Focus on specific areas like time, problem solving, communication, getting house and yard chores done, love, appreciation, acceptance, spending money well, getting along with siblings and stepsiblings, responding to criticism and compliments, and other areas that concern your family.

I'll do what is just by _____ .

WHAT'S A KID LIKE ME DOING IN A FAMILY LIKE THIS?

I'll show constant love by ―――――――――――― .

I'll live in humble fellowship with God by ――――――

――――――――――――――――――――――――――― .

☞ [HINT: Guide group members to suggest specific ways to obey God in areas of family life by making 30-second speeches. Instruct each to choose an area from the above paragraph or from their own experiences and to speak for 30 seconds on how to act justly, show constant love, and live in fellowship with God in that area. Encourage specific actions and attitudes. If group members become anxious, point out the brevity of the speech and that the speeches are more like conversation than a formal presentation. Also explain that brief speeches encourage everyone to talk.]

Select another Bible verse or verses that teach you about spirituality. Your own favorite verses and the following suggestions can get you started:
- Philippians 1:6; 2:13; 4:4-9;
- Hebrews 11:1;
- James 1:22, 26-27;
- 1 John 4:7.

☞ [HELP: Philippians 1:6 – God who began the good work in you will continue it; Philippians 2:13 – God is at work in you for His purposes; Philippians 4:4-9 – Rejoice in knowing God, pray instead of worrying, think about right things; Hebrews 11:1 – Faith is confidence that God will do what He says He will; James 1:22 – Obey God's Word, don't just listen to it; James 1:26-27 – Show your faith through the words and actions you use; 1 John 4:7 – Love people with God's love.]

☞ [HINT: As group members add their own favorite Bible verses, they teach each other.]

How Well We Do

Ponder your own obedience to Micah 6:8; James 1:22; and other Bible passages. Begin by placing your own initials along each continuum. Circle your initials. Then add the initials of each family member.

Hypocrisy .... Christian commitment
Token attendance .... Service at church
Christian talk .... Spiritual actions
Talk of care .... Show care
Pharisaical criticism .... Christlike encouragement
Know all the right answers .... Obedience to Jesus

☞ [HELP: Recall that the Pharisees felt they were best at spirituality and looked down their noses at anyone who didn't meet their standards. On the other hand, Jesus always encouraged people to grow in obedience to God.]

☞ [HINT: Divide into cell groups of two or three to share rankings. Guide the process by circulating as you give instructions for all the groups.]

Where are you in relation to other family members? Rather than smugly declare yourself more holy than your family, or feel inadequate because a family member is miles ahead of you, get growing. How might other family members' actions motivate you to grow more spiritually (either by negative example or positive example)? Recall that spiritual means obedient to Christ. Name one way each family member could teach you about spirituality.

Family member   *Positive/negative example
                          and how it motivates me*

How might your actions help family members to grow spiritually?

☞ **[HINT: As group members share, help them recognize the mutuality of their families. They have responsibilities to help family members grow in Christ and family members have responsibilities to help them grow.]**

大 BODYLIFE
Family of Christ Blessings

Sometimes all it takes to live your faith is the encouragement to do so through words or example. Hopefully your parents give you this encouragement. Encouragement to find and live God's truth might be called giving a blessing. In the Old Testament the parent's blessing frequently imparted acceptance, happiness, and approval. It sometimes served as a prophecy for the future (Genesis 27:27-40). Your parents may bless you with their actions and words. Or they may reject you and your faith expressions. They may do a combination of both. Write or draw a blessing your parent or another family member has given you.

How does this blessing (or lack of it) motivate you to obey Jesus daily?

If your parents don't bless you or don't bless you enough, your brothers and sisters in Christ can become the ones who bless you. You can do the same for them. As a replacement or supplement for your family's blessings, write a specific blessing for each group member.

Name   *Blessing*

☞ **[HELP: Encourage group members to be very specific. Assure them they can bless in more than one way. For example: "May your family always be as 'Cleaverish' as it is now, and may you marry someone with whom life is always an adventure."]**

☞ **[HINT:** Let this blessing process guide the group to experience the love of the body of Christ. Point out the family nature of the church. Ask: How does the body of Christ enhance the family? The family enhance the body of Christ?**]**

Life Response

How do your parents' obedience to God—or lack of obedience—impact you? How can you live your commitment to God in either circumstance? How well are you doing so far?

Whether your parents are uncommitted or deeply committed to God, whether they express that commitment well or poorly, you can decide to deepen your personal spiritual commitment in response.

Read Philippians 4:12-13 and Romans 8:28-39. How do these two passages speak to your own family situation?

How might you grow in Christ in each of the following family case studies? Identify something easy about the situation, something hard, and a specific action you think God would want you to do.

#1 Pam's dad goes to church every time the door is open. She's heard him called a pillar of the church, always serving. At home it's a different story; he has no energy left for listening to Pam or helping her through her problems. He assumes the church needs him more than Pam does. Pam feels he has the image of faith but doesn't show faith at home.

Something easy:

Something hard:

Specific action to grow spiritually:

WHAT'S A KID LIKE ME DOING IN A FAMILY LIKE THIS?

☞ **[HINT: Encourage group members to add details to each story to make it more closely match their families or others they know of.]**

#2 Greg's parents participate in church services twice a week and then reserve the other nights for family commitments. Each parent teaches a class at church and serves on one committee. They encourage Greg to serve in the youth group but not feel like he must go to everything. When Greg asks advice or his parents solve their own problems, Greg hears them mention wanting to do what God wants. They talk about God as friend rather than some holy guy in the sky. Greg feels like they really live what they believe.

Something easy:

Something hard:

Specific action to grow spiritually:

☞ **[HELP: This situation sounds perfect. It is the best of the case studies, but has its hard parts. Greg may feel he'll never reach his parents' level of consistent obedience. He may have doubts he needs to harmonize. Point out that no family is perfect. All provide opportunity for growth in Christ.]**

#3 Louis' dad grew up in church but doesn't go any more. He says faith is fine when you're young, but he doesn't need it now. He's tolerant of Louis' faith, assuming he'll grow out of it when he's ready. Louis is grateful his dad accepts his faith but wishes he'd see it as a sign of manhood, not a precursor to it.

Something easy:

Something hard:

Specific action to grow spiritually:

I'LL TELL YOU WHAT MY PARENTS THINK ABOUT GOD

#4 Beth's mom is angry at God. She blames Him for the divorce that left her, Beth, and Beth's brother with little means of support. Sometimes she assumes God doesn't even exist. Beth sees God as the anchor who keeps her steady in all the chaos of life. She tries to help her mom trust God too, but Beth's mom will have nothing to do with Him.

Something easy:

Something hard:

Specific action to grow spiritually:

#5 Your home: _____

_____

_____

_____

_____

Something easy:

Something hard:

Specific action to grow spiritually:

My Commitment to Obey Christ in My Family
Review the six meetings we've shared on family. Write or illustrate discoveries you've made.

Now combine your discoveries into a commitment to grow happiness in your family. Using the following sample, write a family commitment of your own on a separate sheet of paper. Tape or clip it inside your Bible.

> **COMMITMENT**
>
> God, because you are my ultimate security, I vow to grow more deeply spiritual in my family (Sessions 4 and 6). To do this I will . . .
> - work through little irritations with love (Session 1).
> - appreciate the good we have in our family (Sessions 4 and 5).
> - work together with my parents to set expectations we agree on (Session 2).
> - communicate clearly and compassionately with every member of my family (Session 3).
> - accept my parents and other family members as persons of worth created in the image of God (Session 5).
>
> Bible promises I will depend on include Micah 6:8, _____, and _____.
>
> Signed: _____

☞ [HELP: Additional Life Responses to include if time allows or to suggest for home follow-through:

1. Study a book that develops you spiritually, such as *Making Jesus Lord* or *Influencing Your World* by Barry St. Clair or *It's How You Play the Game* by Duffy Robbins or *Cross Training* by Jane Vogel (all from Victor Books).

2. Observe families in your congregation. How do the parents' interactions with family members show or belie spirituality? How do the children's or teens' interactions with other members show or belie spirituality? Choose at least one family to imitate.

3. What is God's will for you in your family? How will you obey Him?]

LEADER'S EVALUATION SHEET

What's a Kid Like Me Doing in a Family Like This?

Please take a minute to fill out and mail this form giving us your candid reaction to this material. Thanks for your help!

In what setting did you use this Small Group Study? (Sunday School, youth group, midweek Bible study, etc.) _____

How many young people were in your group? _____

What was the age range of those in your group? _____

How long was your average meeting? _____

Do you plan to use other SonPower Small Group Studies? _____ Why or why not?

Did you and your young people enjoy this study? _____ Why or why not?

What are the strengths and/or weaknesses of this leader's edition?

What are the strengths and/or weaknesses of the student book?

Would you like more information on SonPower Youth Sources?

Name	_____
Church name	_____
Church address	_____
	_____
Church phone	(_____)_____
Church size	_____

SGY05

PLACE
STAMP
HERE

SonPower Youth Sources Editor
Victor Books
1825 College Avenue
Wheaton, Illinois 60187